FOOTBALL MAZES

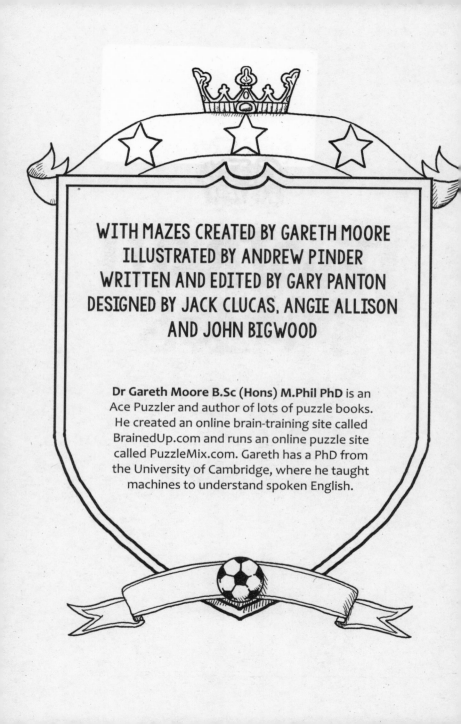

WITH MAZES CREATED BY GARETH MOORE
ILLUSTRATED BY ANDREW PINDER
WRITTEN AND EDITED BY GARY PANTON
DESIGNED BY JACK CLUCAS, ANGIE ALLISON
AND JOHN BIGWOOD

Dr Gareth Moore B.Sc (Hons) M.Phil PhD is an Ace Puzzler and author of lots of puzzle books. He created an online brain-training site called BrainedUp.com and runs an online puzzle site called PuzzleMix.com. Gareth has a PhD from the University of Cambridge, where he taught machines to understand spoken English.

CRAZY MAZEY

FOOTBALL MAZES

Buster Books

First published in Great Britain in 2019 by Buster Books,
an imprint of Michael O'Mara Books Limited,
9 Lion Yard, Tremadoc Road, London SW4 7NQ

 www.mombooks.com/buster Buster Books @BusterBooks

Puzzles and solutions © Gareth Moore 2019
Illustrations and layouts © Buster Books 2019

A CIP catalogue record for this book is available
from the British Library.

ISBN: 978-1-78055-666-6

2 4 6 8 10 9 7 5 3 1

Papers used by Buster Books are natural, recyclable products made
from wood grown in sustainable forests. The manufacturing processes
conform to the environmental regulations of the country of origin.

Printed and bound in October 2019 by CPI Group (UK) Ltd,
108 Beddington Lane, Croydon, CR0 4YY, United Kingdom

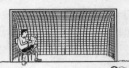

CONTENTS

ARE YOU A-MAZE-ING?

ANSWERS

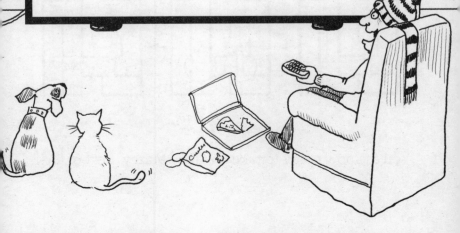

ARE YOU A-MAZE-ING?

Mazes come in all shapes and sizes. In this book, some are circular, some are square, and some come in much odder shapes like football boots, referee's whistles or even half-time snacks.

The mazes inside get tougher as you progress through the levels. With some, you need to dodge obstacles blocking your way. With others, there are items you need to pass by. And trickiest of all are the fiendish bridge mazes, conquered only by true maze-masters (but don't worry – you're about to become one!). With each one, if you're not sure where to start, just follow the arrows.

BRIDGE MAZES

The bridges in these mazes work just like bridges in real life: you can go over them, or you can go under them. Have a look at this example, which shows how they work.

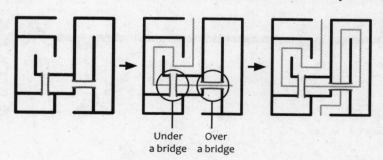

Under a bridge   Over a bridge

You are now ready to take on Crazy Mazey. Best of luck!

LEVEL ONE:

CHAMPIONSHIP

MAZE 1

Find the way through this wall maze before your grumpy neighbour gets even more upset.

MAZE 2

MAZE 3

Sam is a master when it comes to winning headers. Can you master this maze?

MAZE 4

DID YOU KNOW?

The first ever World Cup was in 1930,
and was both hosted and won by Uruguay.

☻

Sixty-one years later, in 1991, China hosted the
first Women's World Cup, which was won by USA.

☻

Spanish lower league side Mostoles Balompie
changed its name to Flat Earth FC in 2019,
in support of the unusual theory that the
Earth is a flat disc rather than a globe.

☻

William Foulke was the heaviest
ever England player. The goalie, who played
for his country in 1897, weighed 140kg.

MAZE 5

This attacker is making a surging run towards
goal, but has got a bit lost. Can you help him out?

MAZE 6

MAZE 7

These best friends are off on a road trip to cheer their team on. Let's hope they don't get lost on the way.

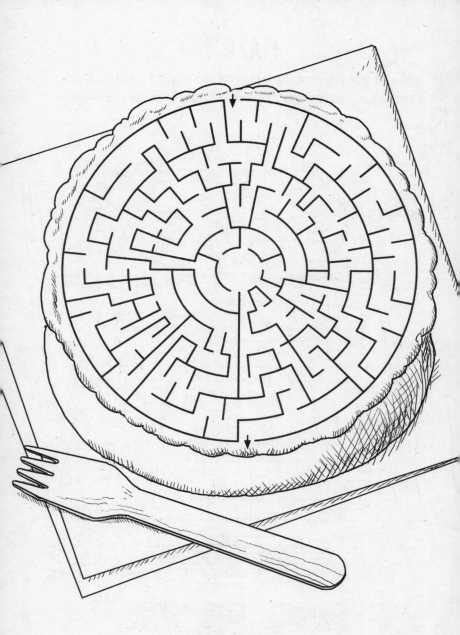

MAZE 8

Can you make it through this juicy half-time pie?

MAZE 9

These fans have bought themselves a massive maze flag.
See if you can spot the way through.

DID YOU KNOW?

Roger Milla, of Cameroon, became the oldest player
to score a goal at a World Cup when he found the
net against Russia at USA '94. He was 42, but
could still wiggle his hips with the best of them,
as he proved with his famous goal celebration.

☻

Sheffield FC are the world's first, and oldest,
football club. They were founded way back in 1857.

☻

In 1921, the English FA banned women
from playing at Football League grounds.
It took 50 years for the ban to be lifted.

☻

Brazil legend Pelé scored an incredible 1,279
goals during his 19-year career. That works
out at an average of over 67 goals a year!

MAZE 10

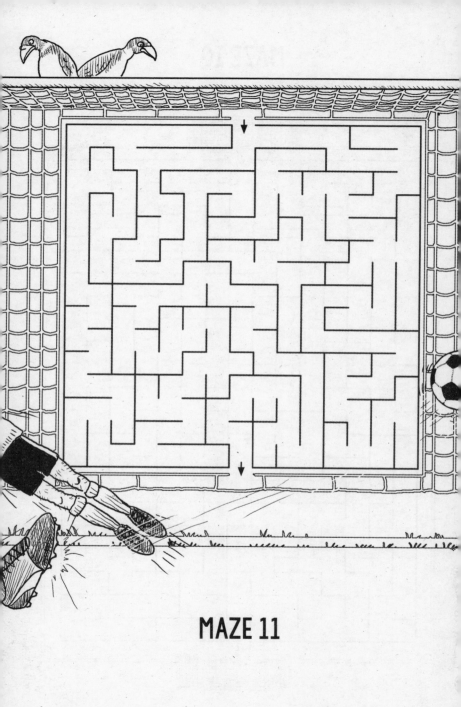

MAZE 11

MAZE 12

Find your way through this snowy soccer scene.

MAZE 13

The big match is about to start on TV. Find the
route through Zane's brand-new flatscreen.

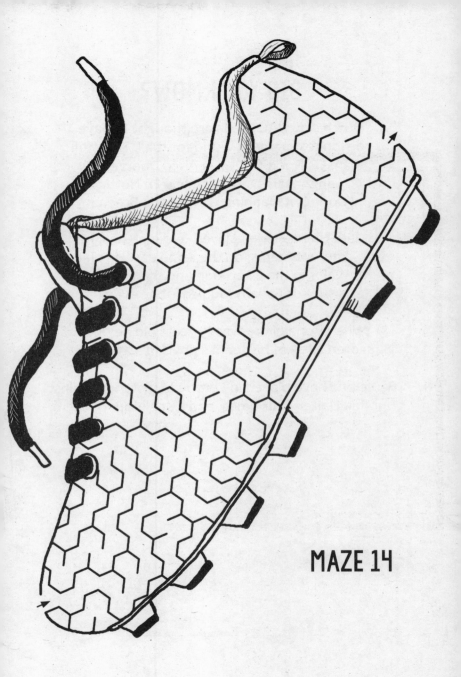

MAZE 14

DID YOU KNOW?

Dutch side NAC Breda are thought to have
the longest name in world football. Their full
name is Nooit Opgeven Altijd Doorzetten
Aangenaam Door Vermaak En Nuttig
Door Ontspanning Combinatie Breda.

⚽

Mark Hughes once played two matches, for
two different teams, on the same day. He played
for Wales in the afternoon and then came on
as a sub for Bayern Munich in the evening.

⚽

When Ronaldinho was 13 years old he once
scored all 23 of his team's goals in a 23-0 win.

⚽

Barcelona have played in European matches against
Dundee United four times, and lost all four of them.

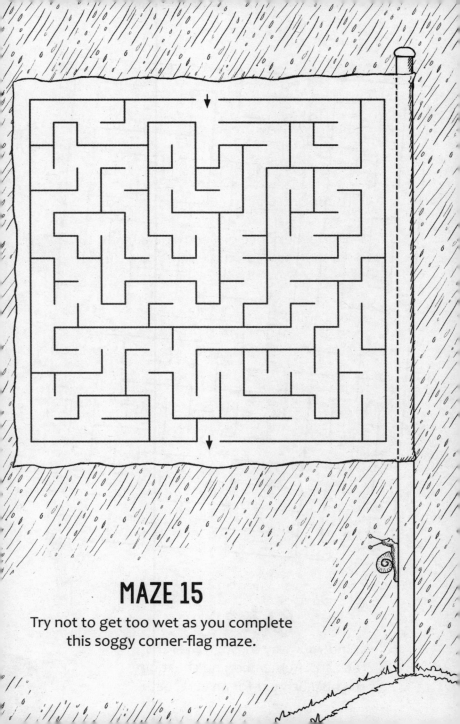

MAZE 15

Try not to get too wet as you complete
this soggy corner-flag maze.

MAZE 16

Find your way through the ref's
red card. Remember: no cheating,
or you'll be next for an early bath.

MAZE 17

These fans have arrived early to get to their favourite seats. Help them complete the maze on the back of the stand while they wait for the match to start.

MAZE 18

LEVEL TWO:
PREMIER LEAGUE

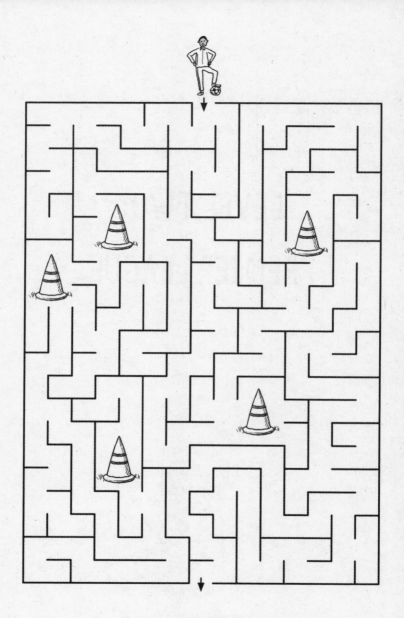

MAZE 19

Use your dribbling skills to avoid
the cones and complete the maze.

MAZE 20

It's prawn sandwich time
up in the director's box.
Can you find the finish?

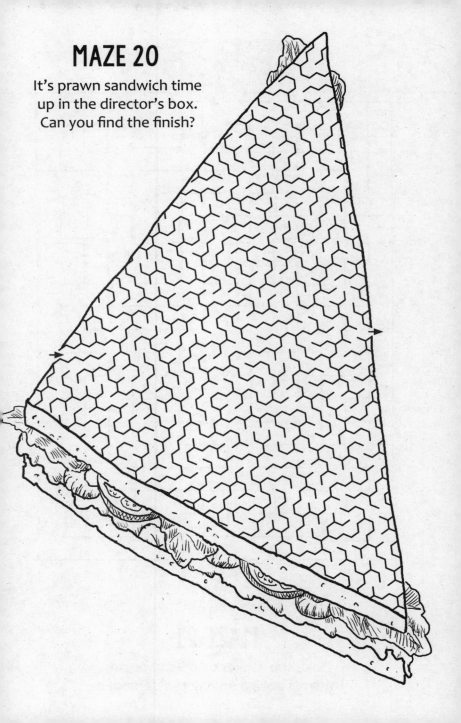

MAZE 21

Take this striker on a winding run
towards goal, avoiding the defenders.

MAZE 22

Poor Alexis has a nasty head injury.
Can you complete the maze on
his extra-large bandage?

DID YOU KNOW?

Chelcee Grimes must go down as one of the most multi-talented footballers. As well as having played women's football for Everton, Spurs and Fulham, she has written songs for loads of pop stars including Kylie Minogue, Olly Murs and Dua Lipa. She also has her own recording career, and has been a football presenter for the BBC.

⚽

In the 1980 Spanish Cup Final, Real Madrid played against their own reserve side, and won 6-1.

⚽

The first ever player to move clubs for over £1 million was Italian striker Giuseppe Savoldi, who signed for Napoli for £1.2 million in 1975.

⚽

When the World Cup trophy was stolen in 1966, a heroic dog named Pickles came to the rescue and found it. Pickles' collar is proudly displayed in England's National Football Museum to this day.

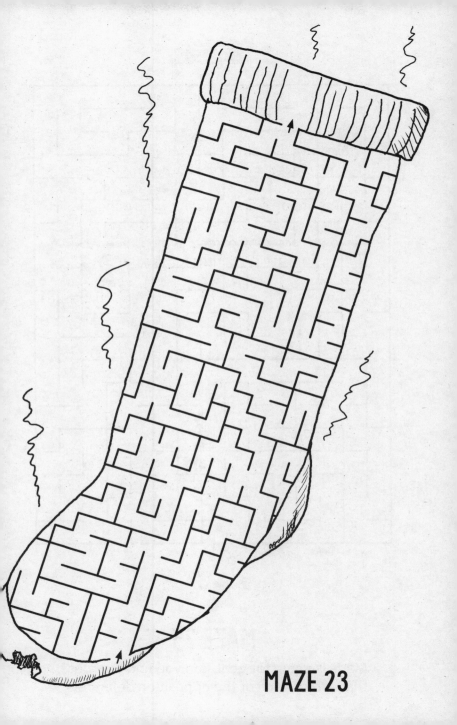

MAZE 23

MAZE 24

Maria is going for goal. Can you find the route
that avoids each of the opposition defenders?

MAZE 25

MAZE 26

This dedicated scout goes out in all weather
to search for new talent. Help take his mind
off the rain by solving his jacket maze.

MAZE 27

DID YOU KNOW?

Adidas are famously the brand with three stripes, but at the 1974 World Cup Johan Cruyff wore his own special two-striped Netherlands kit. He refused to wear Adidas' three stripes because he was sponsored by rival sportswear firm Puma.

✪

When Yugoslavia were disqualified from Euro '92, Denmark took their place with less than two weeks' notice – and went on to win the whole tournament.

✪

The first ever official women's football match took place in 1895 in London. The teams were simply called 'North' and 'South', and North won 7-1.

✪

Celtic were the first British team to win the European Cup (now known as the Champions League), back in 1967. Their entire team was born within 30 miles of their stadium in Glasgow.

MAZE 28

A cat has got on to this team's pitch, and ball
boy Jay has been asked to catch it before kick-off.
Help him find the best route to sneak up on it from.

MAZE 29

MAZE 30

Help this injured midfielder pass
the time until he's fit again by
completing the maze on his cast.

MAZE 31

These fans are pretty unhappy about something.
Maybe the maze has got them stumped?

MAZE 32

This striker is very pleased with his new maze tattoo, but he's left-handed so needs some help completing it.

DID YOU KNOW?

Pelé is the youngest player ever to lift the World Cup.
He was just 17 when his team, Brazil, won it in 1958.

⚽

Finland's Jari Litmanen played international
football in four different decades. He won
his first cap in 1989 and his last in 2010.

⚽

Former Cameroon player Alex Song is one of
28 siblings. He has 17 brothers and 10 sisters!

⚽

France defender Laurent Blanc kissed the bald head
of goalkeeper Fabien Barthez before their matches
at the 1998 World Cup. When Blanc had to miss the final
through suspension, teammate Frank Leboeuf puckered
up instead, and France won the tournament.

MAZE 33

MAZE 35

Solve the maze to make your way
from one match ticket to the other.

MAZE 36

Find your way through the mascot's massive shirt.

MAZE 37

Can you get from one side of
this deflated ball to the other?

MAZE 38

MAZE 39

These beach ballers are having fun in the sun.
Can you get through the sandy maze?

DID YOU KNOW?

Italian giants Juventus used to play in pink but changed to black and white stripes in 1903 after having a set of kits gifted to them by Notts County.

⚽

Ex-Arsenal manager Arsène Wenger has an asteroid named after him.

⚽

The Isles of Scilly boast the smallest football league in the world. It has just two teams, who play against each other every week.

⚽

An incredible 36 red cards were shown in one match between Argentinean clubs Claypole and Victoriano Arenas in 2011. Both teams had their players, substitutes and even coaches sent off after a huge brawl on the pitch.

MAZE 40

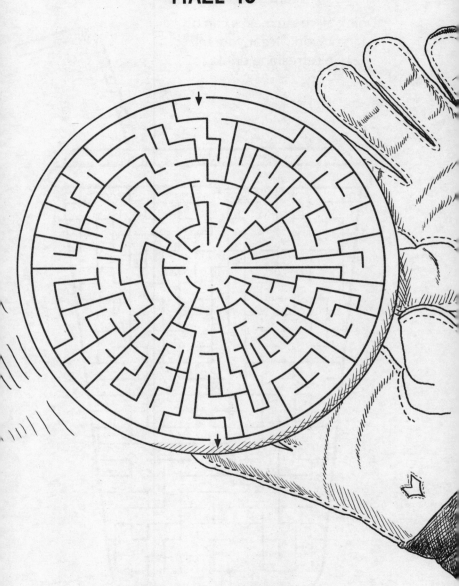

MAZE 41

Doing all these mazes can be
thirsty work. Treat yourself
to a refreshing drink.

MAZE 42

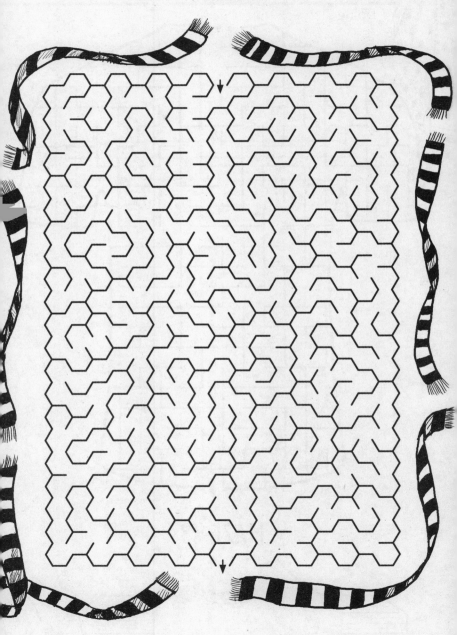

MAZE 43

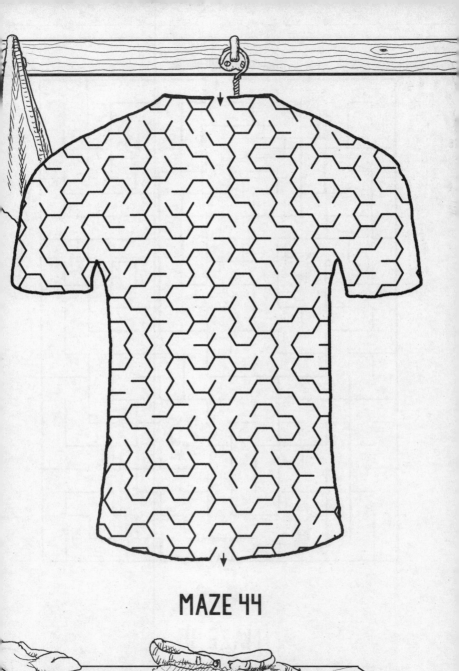

MAZE 44

MAZE 45

Help this wing wizard dribble the ball all the way to goal,
avoiding the defenders along the way.

MAZE 46

DID YOU KNOW?

The 2018 World Cup Final was watched
by 3.5 billion viewers, which is more than
half the population of the entire planet.

⚽

Giuseppe Bergomi played for Italy in four
World Cups between 1982 and 1998, but
never appeared in a single qualifying match.

⚽

The British Ladies' Football Club, which was the
first official women's football club, was founded
in 1874 by the brilliantly named Nettie Honeyball.
Sadly, it's thought that this was a false name
and she was really called Mary Hutson.

⚽

Cristiano Ronaldo has his own museum
in Madeira, where many of his trophies,
medals and shirts are on display.

MAZE 47

Angelo has been voted as having the best hair in world football for six years in a row. Find your way through his latest awesome hairdo.

MAZE 48

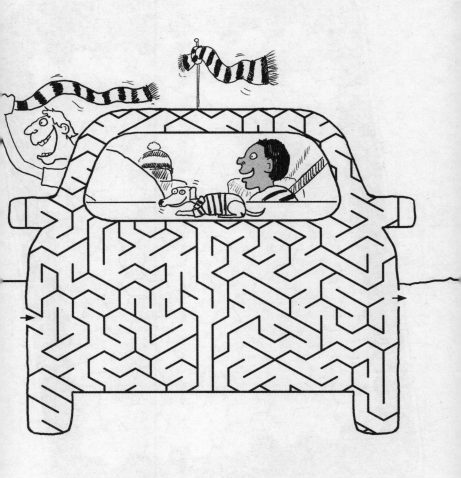

MAZE 49

MAZE 50

Jermain the manager's phone won't stop
buzzing. He tells everyone he's getting calls from
agents, but really it's alerts from his maze app.

MAZE 51

Find a sneaky way through this ticket queue.

MAZE 52

Jakub is going to have a sore
head in the morning. Can you
make it through his football?

LEVEL THREE:

CHAMPIONS LEAGUE

MAZE 53

Complete this maze and then run round and round the room celebrating, just like these fans are doing.

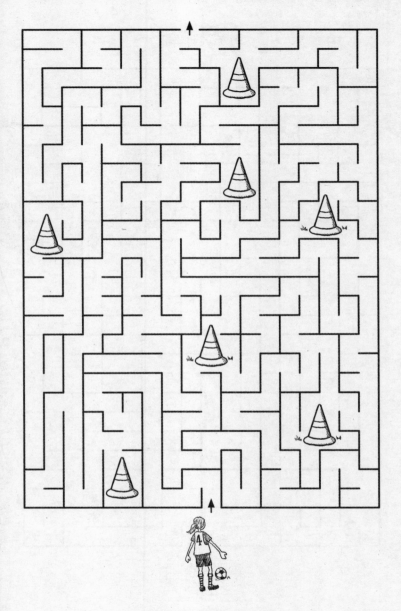

MAZE 54

Help Lena prove she's a dribbler supreme by dodging all of these cones on her way through the maze.

MAZE 55

Can you find a route through the maze that passes by each player on its way to goal?

MAZE 56

Help Max get to the stadium in
time for his team's big match.

DID YOU KNOW?

Nigeria fans have a tradition of bringing
live chickens to matches with them. They
even paint them in their team's green and
white colours. The chickens were
banned from the 2018 World Cup in Russia.

✪

Scottish side St Johnstone are the only senior league
team in Britain who have a letter J in their name.

✪

Usain Bolt is known as one of the greatest athletes
of all time, but he also made a brief attempt at a
football career. After hanging up his running shoes,
the Jamaican legend spent several months on trial
with the Australian team Central Coast Mariners.

✪

When Sunderland signed Swedish midfielder
Stefan Schwarz in 1999, they put a clause in
his contract banning him from space travel.

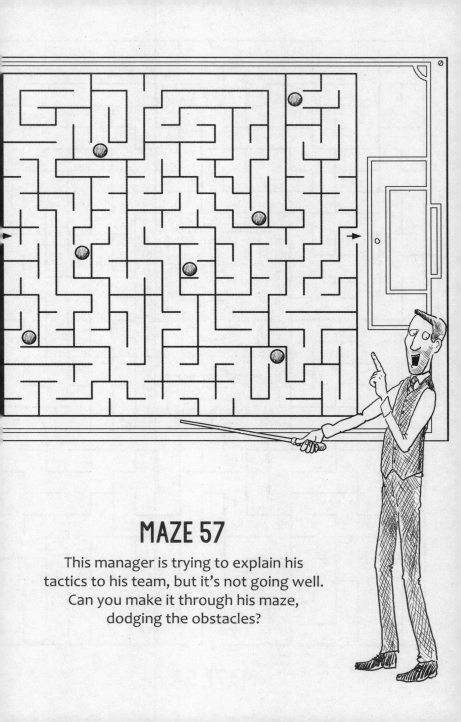

MAZE 57

This manager is trying to explain his
tactics to his team, but it's not going well.
Can you make it through his maze,
dodging the obstacles?

MAZE 58

MAZE 59

The clock is ticking on this referee's watch. Make it to the middle of the maze before he blows for full-time.

MAZE 60

These happy fans have hired a bus to take them
to their team's big away match. Can you make
it from the front of the coach to the back?

MAZE 61

This commentator is running late. Can you help him find his way to the commentary box before he gets in trouble?

MAZE 62

It's Nat's turn to show off her dribbling skills. Help her get around the training pitch, dodging each cone on the way.

DID YOU KNOW?

In a game between Aston Villa and Leicester City
in 1976, Villa defender Chris Nicholl scored an
impressive four goals – but two of them were
own goals with the match finishing 2-2.

☉

The Australia women's team is nicknamed
'The Matildas', after the Australian folk song 'Waltzing
Matilda'. The men's team is known as 'The Socceroos'.

☉

Stamford Bridge stadium in London was originally
offered to Fulham to play in. When they declined,
Chelsea were formed as a new club to play there instead.

☉

During the 1958 World Cup, France striker Just Fontaine
scored an incredible 13 goals in just six matches.

MAZE 63

MAZE 64

MAZE 65

Guide Harry to goal-scoring glory,
avoiding the defenders.

MAZE 66

MAZE 67

Solve the maze on this stadium's floodlight.

DID YOU KNOW?

Luis Figo once had a pig's head thrown at him while playing for Real Madrid against his former team, Barcelona.

⚽

The CONIFA World Cup is competed for by countries and regions that are not members of FIFA. Previous winners include Kárpátalja and Abkhazia.

⚽

Footballers run between 11 and 16km in the average professional match. That's more than in any other team sport.

⚽

Gary Lineker went through his entire playing career without ever being booked.

MAZE 68

This stadium car park is huge!
Can you find your way through?

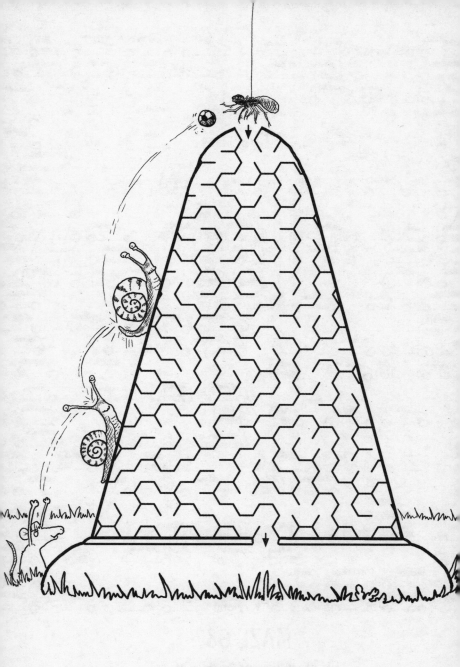

MAZE 69

MAZE 70

MAZE 71

New signing Javier has got lost on his way
to his first day at training. Can you help him out?

MAZE 72

Poor Paul has found himself on the bench, yet again.
Help him solve the maze on his bib to pass the time
while he waits for his chance to get on to the pitch.

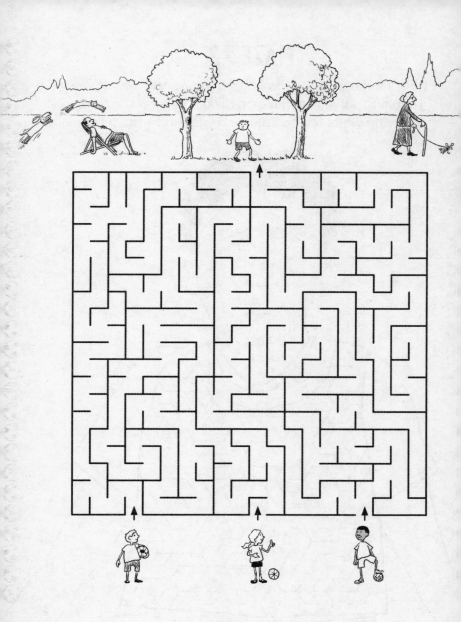

MAZE 73

Kyle, Lorna and Adnan are playing football in the park. Which one scores between the two trees?

MAZE 74

Footballs everywhere! Can you find the path through them?
If you come to a burst one, you have to go back.

DID YOU KNOW?

The highest ever official attendance for a
football match was 199,854, when Brazil played
Uruguay in the 1950 World Cup. It's thought that
a lot of people snuck in without tickets, so the
actual attendance may have been even higher.

⚽

In 1998, Romanian side Valcea bought
midfielder Ion Radu from rival team Jiul Petrosani,
but instead of money changing hands, they
paid with 2,000kg of beef and pork.

⚽

When the 1995 Spanish Cup Final had to be
abandoned due to heavy rain, it was decided
that the teams would return three days later
to play the remaining 11 minutes. When the
match restarted, Deportivo scored instantly
and went on to beat Valencia 2-1.

⚽

During a match in 1975, Manchester United
goalie Alex Stepney yelled at his defence
so much that he dislocated his jaw.

MAZE 75

MAZE 76

Make your way around this
fan's football sticker book.

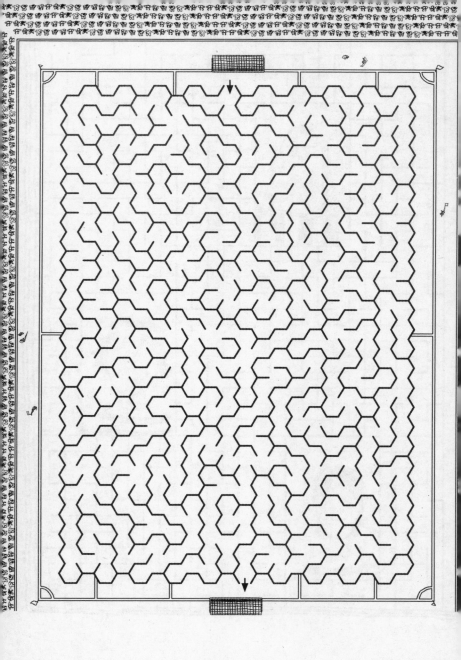

MAZE 77

LEVEL FOUR:
WORLD CUP

MAZE 78

Every four years, players and fans from all
over the planet head to the World Cup.
Have a go at this global maze.

MAZE 79

MAZE 80

MAZE 81

DID YOU KNOW?

In Argentina, Diego Maradona's legendary status is so huge that there is a religion dedicated to worshipping him. Among the religion's commandments are 'spread the news of Diego's miracles throughout the universe' and 'love football above all else'.

☉

The 1999 Women's World Cup was the first ever World Cup to be refereed entirely by women.

☉

A 1996 match between Estonia and Scotland lasted just three seconds – because Estonia didn't turn up. The hosts boycotted the match due to a disagreement over the kick-off time, but Scotland took to the pitch and kicked off anyway.

☉

There was no World Cup in either 1942 or 1946 because of the Second World War.

MAZE 82

Can you make it through this team's proudly displayed trophy cabinet?

MAZE 83

Carlos is a super-fan who is famous for
going to matches in awesome costumes.
See if you can make it all the way across
his latest eye-catching outfit.

MAZE 84

Only one of these players has a
clear route to goal. Which one?

MAZE 85

MAZE 86

Can you find your way to the front row of this big stand? Mind you don't step on anyone's feet as you make your way there.

DID YOU KNOW?

In a 2006 World Cup match against Australia, Croatia's Josip Šimunić was yellow carded three times before finally being sent off. English referee Graham Poll was sent home for making the mistake.

☻

In 2018, Turkish club Gulspor exchanged 18 of their youth players for ten goats, so that they could earn some extra money from selling milk.

☻

In 1979, a Scottish Cup tie between Inverness Thistle and Falkirk had to be postponed 29 times because of bad weather.

☻

Football's Bosman transfer rule is named after Belgian lower league player Jean-Marc Bosman, who took his club to court in 1995 when they wouldn't let him move on at the end of his contract. Players have been moving from club to club 'on a Bosman' ever since.

MAZE 87

These three all have a ball, but only one can make it all the way to goal. Who will find the back of the net?

MAZE 88

MAZE 89

Steve the programme seller needs to get to each
fan before he can finish his shift. Give him a hand.

MAZE 90

Guide this physio to the injured player,
and be quick – it looks like a bad one!

MAZE 91

Make sure Jamal dodges all of these
cones on his way to the finish.

MAZE 92

Rob is working hard in the gym to get fit for next season. Make your way around his gigantic weight.

MAZE 93

Finding your seat is not always easy! Make your way through this crowd without bumping into your fellow fans.

DID YOU KNOW?

Manchester City goalie Bert Trautmann
broke his neck during the 1956 FA Cup Final,
but didn't realize, so played on for the rest
of the match. City went on to win 3-1.

☺

When Atlético Madrid were sponsored by film
studio Columbia Pictures in 2003/04, nearly every
match saw them promote a different movie.
Film titles to appear on their shirts included
Spider-Man, *Peter Pan* and *Bad Boys 2*.

☺

German goalkeeper Lutz Pfannenstiel was the
first person to play professionally for clubs in all six
FIFA confederations (Asia, Africa, North/Central
America, South America, Oceania and Europe).

☺

Andy Goram played for Scotland at two
different sports – football and cricket.

MAZE 94

Pick up all of the footballs on
your way around the maze.

MAZE 95

Can you solve this mascot maze?

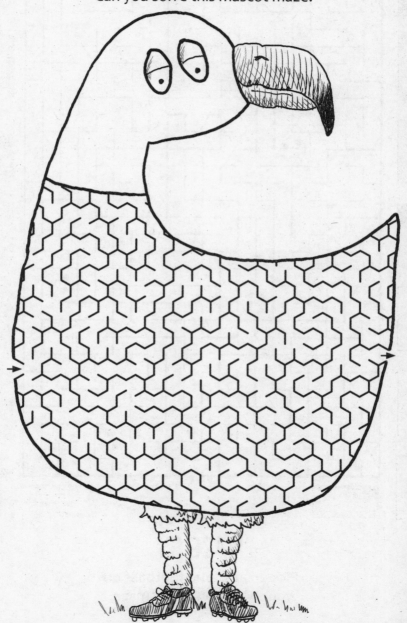

MAZE 96

MAZE 97

Make your way around all four shirt mazes in this dressing room.

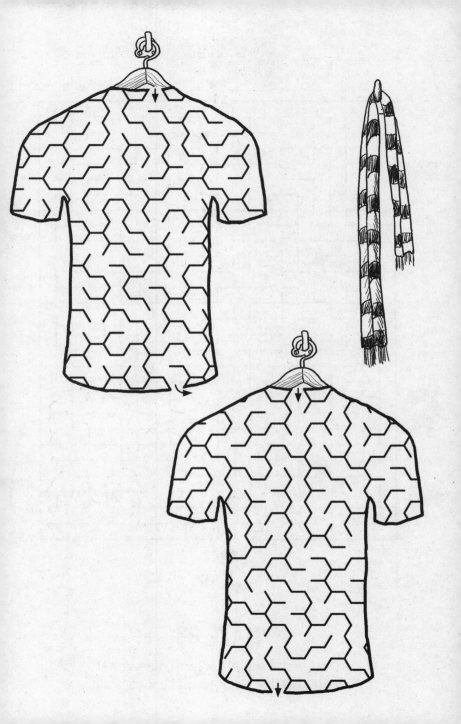

MAZE 98

Dodge the molehills (and occasional
mole) on this pitch to make it to goal.

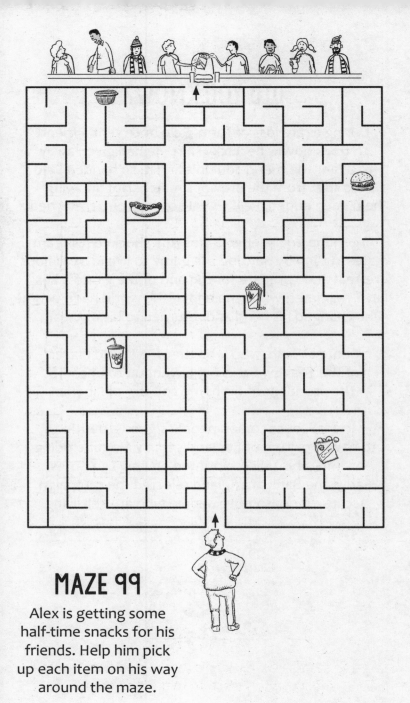

MAZE 99

Alex is getting some half-time snacks for his friends. Help him pick up each item on his way around the maze.

DID YOU KNOW?

During a rare loss of form, Pelé once sent a friend
to track down the 'lucky shirt' he had given away
to a fan. The friend couldn't find it, so handed Pelé
his shirt from the previous match. Not knowing
he'd been duped, Pelé's goal-scoring touch returned.

☻

Argentina goalkeeper Carlos Roa shocked his team
mates in 1999 by quitting the game to live in a religious
retreat and "prepare for the end of the world". Less
than a year later, when the end of the world hadn't come,
he changed his mind and returned to his old team.

☻

George Weah, who won the FIFA World Player
of the Year award in 1995, went on to become
the president of his home country of Liberia.

☻

In 2018, over 50,000 people signed a petition
to have a picture of England's Harry Maguire riding
an inflatable unicorn printed on new £50 notes.
Sadly, the Bank of England rejected the campaign
because it doesn't use people who are still living.

MAZE 100

MAZE 101

MAZE 102

Guide Chris to goal, dodging the defenders on the way.

MAZE 103

Only the all-time greats get their photo put up in the Hall of Fame. Make your way around the pictures of these legends.

DID YOU KNOW?

Gordon Strachan is the only person born before
1960 to have scored a hat-trick in England's
Premier League. He scored it for Leeds
against Blackburn in 1993, at the age of 36.

☻

Nearly half of the world's footballs are
made in the city of Sialkot in Pakistan.

☻

Jimmy Greaves was a hero for England in their 1962
World Cup match against Brazil – for catching a dog
that ran on to the pitch. Brazil star Garrincha was so
taken with the dog that he ended up adopting it.

☻

Mia Hamm is known as one of the greatest
players of all time, despite having been born
with a birth defect known as a clubfoot.
As a child, the USA legend had to wear casts
and special shoes to correct the problem.

MAZE 104

Help tidy up this stadium exit by picking up
each piece of litter on your way out.

MAZE 105

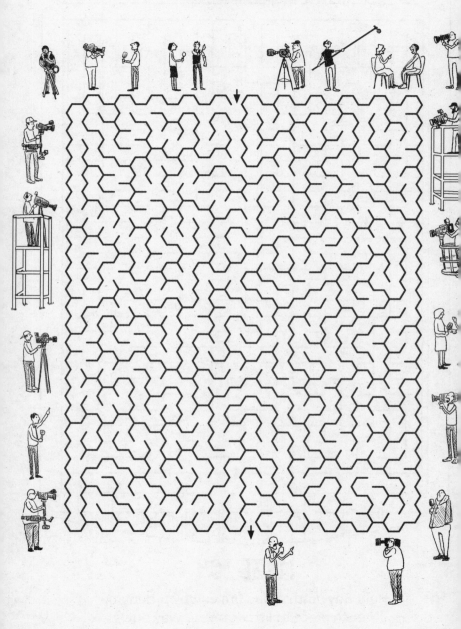

MAZE 106

The defenders in this match are extra-tough to get past. Can you spot a way for Stefan to avoid them on his way to goal?

MAZE 107

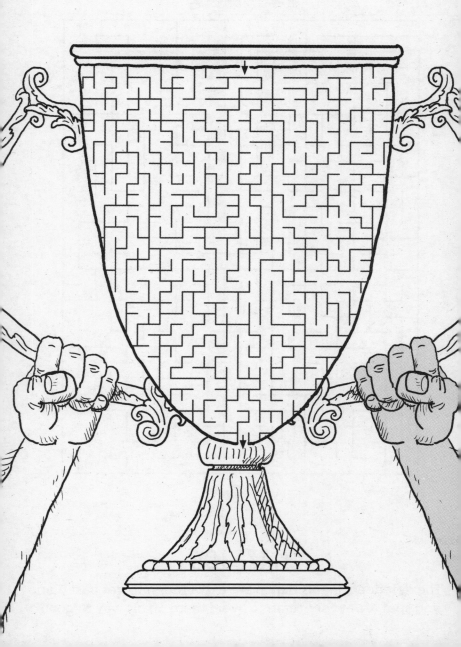

ANSWERS

LEVEL ONE:

CHAMPIONSHIP

MAZE 3

MAZE 1

MAZE 4

MAZE 2

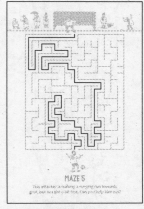

MAZE 5

MAZE 6

MAZE 6

MAZE 9

These fans have bought themselves a massive maze flag.
See if you can spot the way through.

MAZE 9

MAZE 7

These best friends are off on a road trip to cheer their
team on. Let's hope they don't get lost on the way.

MAZE 7

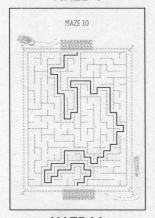

MAZE 10

MAZE 10

MAZE 8

Can you make it through this juicy half-time pie?

MAZE 8

MAZE 11

MAZE 14

MAZE 12

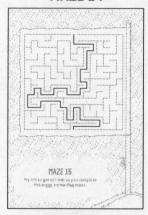

MAZE 15

MAZE 13

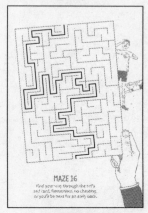

MAZE 16

MAZE 17

These fans have arrived early to get to their favourite seats. Help them complete the maze on the back of the stand while they wait for the match to start.

MAZE 17

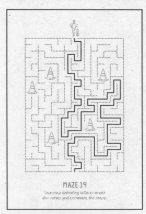

MAZE 19

Use your dribbling skills to avoid the cones and complete this maze.

MAZE 19

MAZE 18

MAZE 18

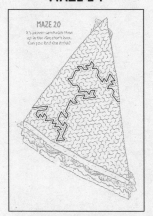

MAZE 20

It's prawn sandwich time up in the director's box. Can you find the fillings?

MAZE 20

LEVEL TWO: PREMIER LEAGUE

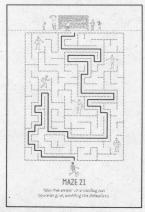

MAZE 21

Take this striker on a winding run towards goal, avoiding the defenders.

MAZE 21

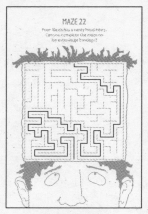

MAZE 22

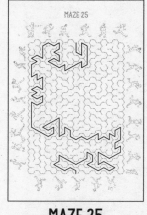

MAZE 25

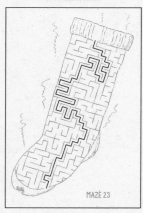

MAZE 23

MAZE 26

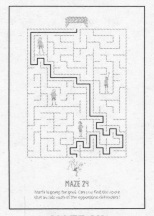

MAZE 24

MAZE 27

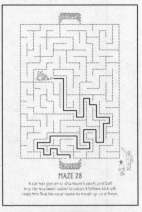

MAZE 28

A cat has got on to this team's pitch, and ball boy Jay has been asked to catch it before kick off. Help him find the best route to sneak up on it from.

MAZE 28

MAZE 31

These fans are pretty unhappy about something. Maybe the maze has got them stumped?

MAZE 31

MAZE 29

MAZE 29

MAZE 32

The sailor is very pleased with his new maze tattoo, but he's left-handed so needs some help completing it.

MAZE 32

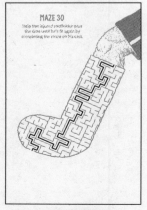

MAZE 30

Help this injured footballer pass the time until he's fit again by completing the maze on his cast.

MAZE 30

MAZE 33

MAZE 33

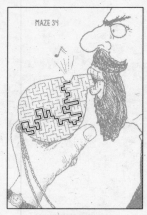

MAZE 34

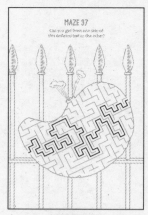

MAZE 37

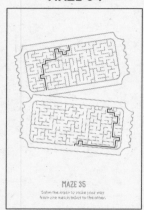

MAZE 35

MAZE 38

MAZE 36

MAZE 39

MAZE 40

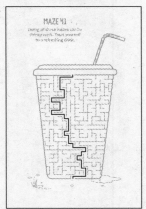

MAZE 41

MAZE 42

MAZE 43

MAZE 44

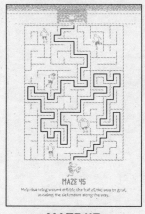

MAZE 45

MAZE 46

MAZE 49

MAZE 49

MAZE 47

Angelo has been voted as having the best hair in world football for six years in a row. Find your way through his latest awesome barnet.

MAZE 47

MAZE 50

Jermain the manager's phone won't stop buzzing. He tells everyone he's getting calls from agents, but really it's alerts from his maze app.

MAZE 50

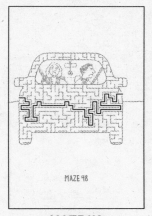

MAZE 48

MAZE 48

MAZE 51

Find a sneaky way through this ticket queue.

MAZE 51

MAZE 52

LEVEL THREE: CHAMPIONS LEAGUE

MAZE 54
Help Lena prove she's a dribbler supreme by dodging all of these cones on her way through the maze.

MAZE 54

MAZE 53
Complete this maze and then run round and round the room celebrating, just like these fans are doing.

MAZE 53

MAZE 55
Can you find a route through the maze that passes by each player on its way to goal?

MAZE 55

MAZE 56

Help Max get to the stadium in time for his team's big match.

MAZE 59

The clock is ticking on the referee's watch. Make it to the middle of the maze before he blows for full time.

MAZE 59

MAZE 57

This manager is trying to explain his tactics to his team, but it's not going well. Can you make it through his maze, dodging the obstacles?

MAZE 57

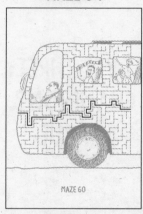

MAZE 60

MAZE 60

MAZE 58

MAZE 58

These happy fans have hired a bus to take them to their team's big away match. Can you make it from the front of the coach to the back?

MAZE 60 (CONT.)

MAZE 61

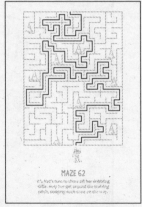

MAZE 62

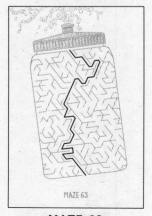

MAZE 63

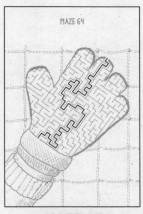

MAZE 64

MAZE 65

MAZE 66

MAZE 67

MAZE 70

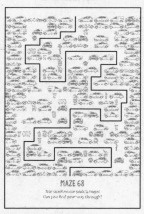

MAZE 68

MAZE 71

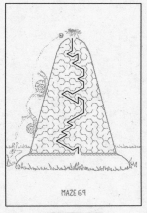

MAZE 69

MAZE 72

MAZE 73

MAZE 76

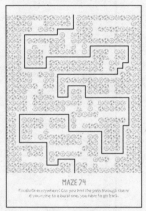

MAZE 74

MAZE 76 (CONT.)

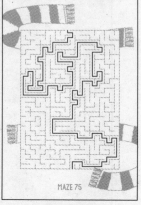

MAZE 75

MAZE 77

LEVEL FOUR: WORLD CUP

MAZE 78

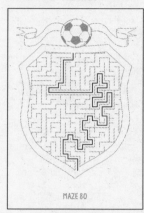

MAZE 80

MAZE 79

MAZE 81

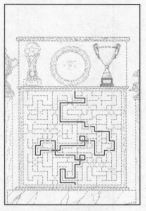

MAZE 82

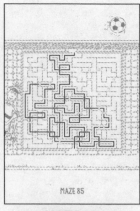

MAZE 85

MAZE 85

MAZE 83

Carlos is a super fan who is famous for going to matches in awesome costumes. See if you can make it all the way across his latest eye-catching outfit.

MAZE 83

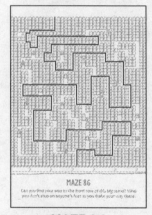

MAZE 86

Can you find your way to the front row of the big game? Make sure you don't step on anyone's feet as you make your way there.

MAZE 86

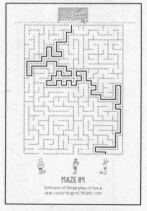

MAZE 84

Only one of these players has a clear route to goal. Which one?

MAZE 84

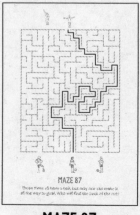

MAZE 87

These three all have a ball, but only one can make it all the way to goal. Who will find the back of the net!

MAZE 87

MAZE 88

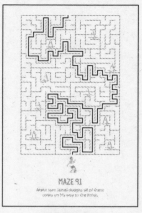

MAZE 91

Make sure Jamal dodges all of these coins on his way to the hotel.

MAZE 91

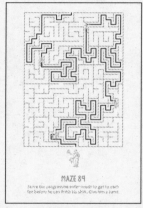

MAZE 89

Solve this programme seller needs to get to each fan before he can finish his shift. Give him a hand.

MAZE 89

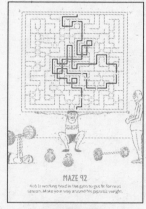

MAZE 92

Rob is working hard in the gym to get fit for next season. Make your way around his gigantic weight.

MAZE 92

MAZE 90

Guide the physio to the injured player, and be quick-y it might be a bad one!

MAZE 90

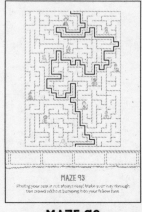

MAZE 93

Finding your seat is not always easy! Make your way through this crowd without bumping into your fellow fans.

MAZE 93

MAZE 94

Pick up all the footballs on
your way around the maze.

MAZE 94

MAZE 95

Can you solve this mascot maze?

MAZE 95

MAZE 96

MAZE 96

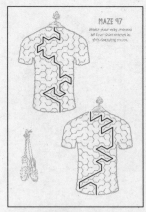

MAZE 97

Work your way around
all four shirt ranges in
this dressing room.

MAZE 97

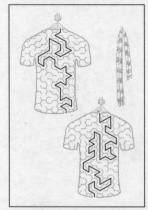

MAZE 97 (CONT.)

MAZE 98

Dodge the molehills (and occasional
moles!) on the pitch to make it to goal.

MAZE 98

MAZE 99

MAZE 100

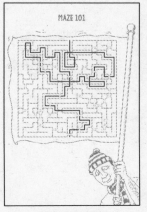

MAZE 101

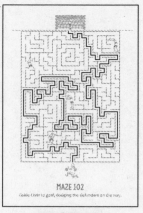

MAZE 102

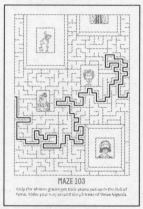

MAZE 103

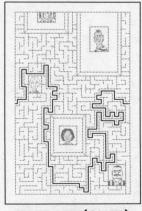

MAZE 103 (CONT.)

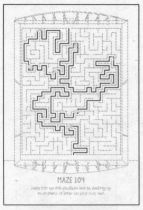

MAZE 104

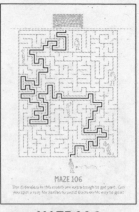

MAZE 106

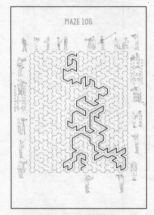

MAZE 105

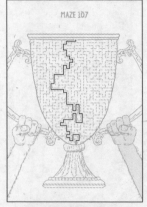

MAZE 107

MORE CRAZY MAZES ...

ISBN: 978-1-178055-667-3